3 Activity Book

T0306630

Pippa and Pop

British English

Colin Sage

with **Caroline Nixon & Michael Tomlinson**

CAMBRIDGE
UNIVERSITY PRESS

Map of the book

	VOCABULARY	LANGUAGE	SOUNDS AND LETTERS	LITERACY AND VALUES	NUMBERS	CROSS-CURRICULAR
Introduction Page 4						
1 Me! Page 6	Review Level 2: characters, numbers, likes *angry, bored, excited, scared, sleepy, surprised*	Hello! What's your name? I'm (Kim). How old are you? I'm (eight). I like (books). What's her / his name? She's (Kim). He's (Dan). How old is she / he? She / He's (eight). He's / She's / I'm (bored). He isn't / She isn't / I'm not (bored).	Review Level 2 letter sounds: *b, m, t, g, p, d, k, n, s, h*	*Jane's name* Be yourself	Review numbers: *1 – 20*	Music: Emotions from music
2 My day Page 18	*brush my hair, brush my teeth, get dressed, have breakfast, wake up, wash my face* *go to bed, have a bath, have dinner, have a snack, listen to a story, play with friends*	I (wake up) (in the morning / every day). They / We (play with friends) (after school / in the evening). We / They don't (have a bath).	Letter sound /ʃ/ (sh)	*Brush your hair, Leo!* Look after yourself	Adding up by counting	Social studies: Times of day
3 My home Page 30	*make the bed, pick up the toys, set the table, sweep the floor, wash the clothes, wash the dishes* *bed, bookcase, cupboard, lamp, rug, toy box*	He / She (washes the dishes). I (sweep the floor). It's (under / in / on / next to) the (bed).	Letter sound / **k** / (ck)	*Goldilocks and the three bears* Respect other people's things	Numbers: *10, 20, 30, 40*	Social studies: Objects at home
Units 1–3 Review Page 42–43						
4 My sports Page 44	*badminton, baseball, basketball, football, hockey, tennis* *bouncing, catching, hitting, kicking, rolling, throwing*	They're / She's / He's playing (football). She's / He's / They're / I'm (throwing) the ball.	Letter sound /ŋ/ (ng)	*A sport for Grace* Persevere	Subtracting by counting	Physical education: Team sports

	VOCABULARY	LANGUAGE	SOUNDS AND LETTERS	LITERACY AND VALUES	NUMBERS	CROSS-CURRICULAR
5 **My free time** Page 56	cooking dinner, drawing pictures, listening to music, playing video games, reading books, watching TV go roller skating, go swimming, play a board game, play with building blocks, play hide-and-seek, play outside	I / We like (reading books). Let's (go swimming / play a board game)! Can I (come / play)?	Letter sounds / ʊ / (short oo) and / uː / (long oo)	Jack loves reading Join in and help	Numbers: 50, 60	Art: Paintings, photographs and sculptures
6 **My food** Page 68	cake, chocolate, crisps, grapes, pineapple, sweets beans, cereal, fruit, meat, rice, vegetables	Would you like some (chocolate)? Yes, please. / No, thank you. I'd like some (sweets), please. I / We have (meat and rice) for (breakfast / lunch / dinner).	Letter sound / tʃ / (ch)	Share, Ricky Raccoon! Share	Estimating quantity	Science: Salty, sour and sweet
Units 4–6 Review Page 80–81						
7 **Animals** Page 82	crocodile, elephant, hippo, monkey, snake, tiger duck, giraffe, lizard, parrot, spider, zebra	There's (a monkey). There are (three) (monkeys). There are (lots of) (snakes). They're (giraffes). They've got (long necks / long legs / stripes / short legs / big feet / long tails / sharp teeth). They're (fast).	Letter sound / θ / (th)	The mouse and the lion Be friendly	Numbers: 70, 80	Science: Where animals live
8 **Plants** Page 94	garden, plants, rain, seeds, soil, sun beautiful, clean, dirty, new, old, ugly	What do plants need? Plants need (sun / rain / soil). What (beautiful) (flowers)! What (a dirty) (nose)!	Letter sound / iː / (ee, ea)	Sophia's garden Work together	Measuring length	Science: How plants grow
9 **My town** Page 106	hospital, playground, restaurant, school, shop, supermarket doctor, farmer, nurse, shop assistant, teacher, waiter	Where are you / we going? I'm / We're going to the (supermarket). A (teacher) works in a (school). He / She works on a farm. Where does (a teacher) work? Does (a nurse) work (in) a (hospital)? Yes, he / she does. No, he / she doesn't.	Letter sound / eɪ / (ay, ai)	Big-city cat and small-town cat Appreciate what you have	Numbers: 90, 100	Social studies: Jobs
Units 7–9 Review Page 118–119						

Hello again!

⊙ Look. 🔍 Find. ◯ Circle.

👁 Look. 📖 Match. 💬 Say.

Me!

🎧 3 **Listen again.** 👁 **Look.** 🔵 **Stick.** 👆 **Point.**

1 **Unit topic introduction:** Song practice

👁 Look. ✋ Count. 📓 Match. 💬 Say.

At home Ask a friend *What's your name? How old are you?*

Language review: *What's your name? I'm (Dan). How old are you? I'm (five).* 1 7

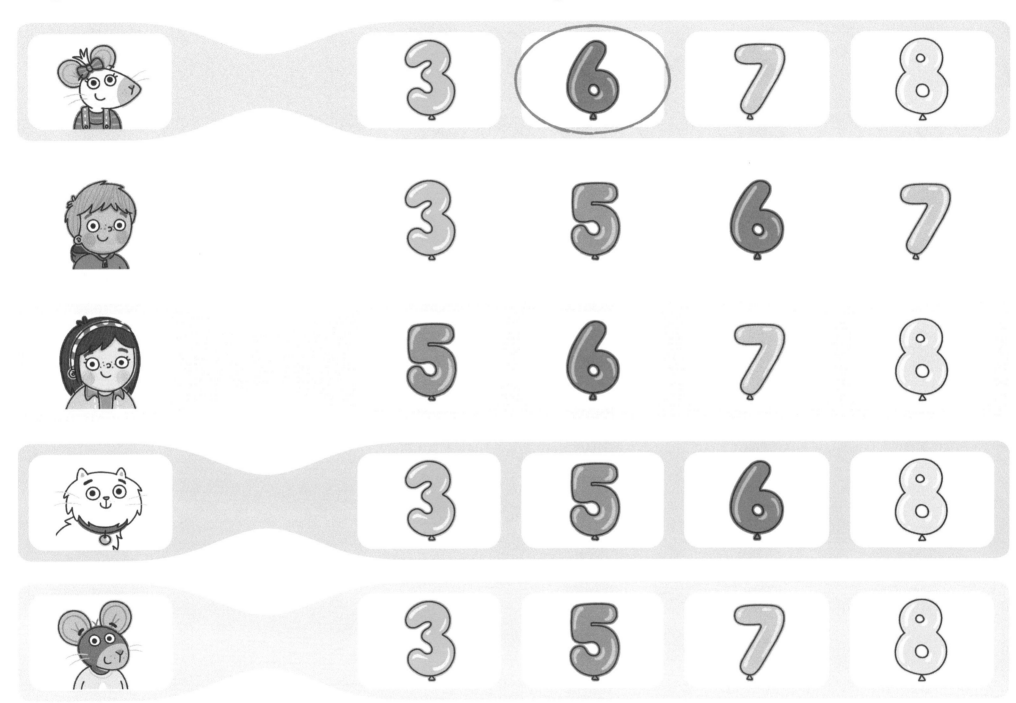 Look. 🔍 Find. ○ Circle. 💬 Say.

1 Language practice: *What's your / her / his name? I'm / She's / He's (Pippa / Dan / Kim / Tinks / Pop). How old are you / is she / is he? I'm / He's / She's (six / five / eight / three).*

🎧 **Listen again.** 👁 **Look.** ⭕ **Circle.** 💬 **Say.**

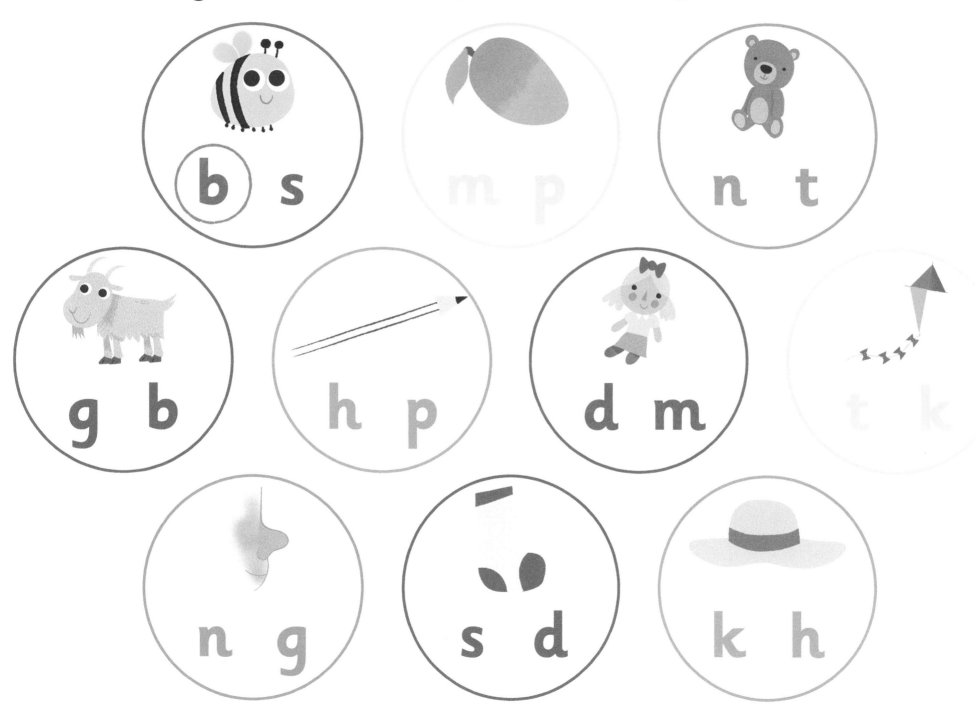

👁 Look. 👆 Point. ⭕ Circle.

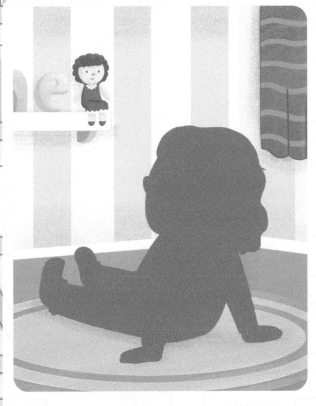

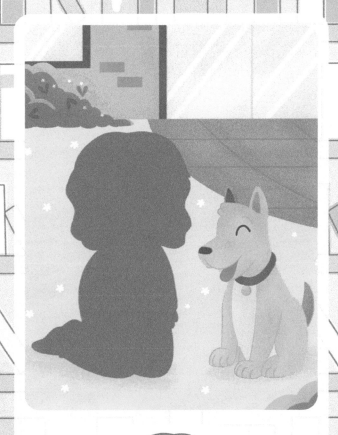

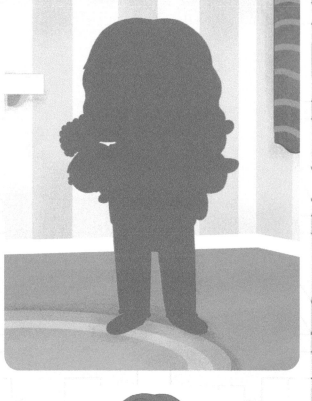

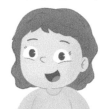

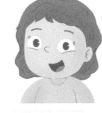

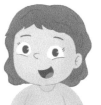

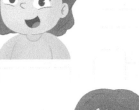

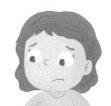

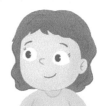

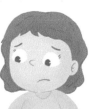

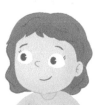

10 1 Literacy practice: Jane's name

👁 Look. 🔍 Find. ✏ Draw.

🏠 **At home**

What do you like about yourself?

⊙ Look. 🔍 Find. ⭕ Circle. 💬 Say.

1 **Vocabulary practice:** *excited, sleepy, angry, surprised, scared, bored*

👁 Look. 🔍 Find. 📖 Match. 💬 Say.

👁 **Look.** ✏️ **Draw.** ✋ **Count.** 💬 **Say.**

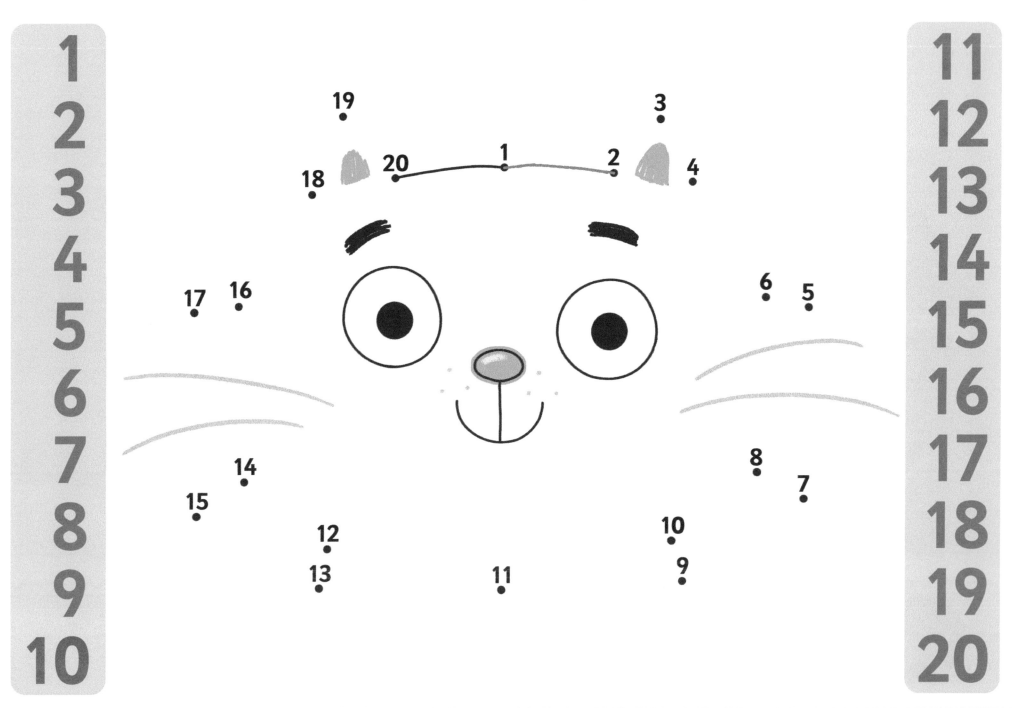

⌖ ¹⁰ Listen again. ✏ Draw.

⌂ **At home** Listen to some music together. Say how it makes you feel.

Emotions from music 1 15

 **Look.** **Draw.** **Say.**

1 *I'm / She's / He's (surprised). I'm not / He isn't / She isn't (bored).*

 Point. 💬 Say. ✏️ Draw.

Well done!

What's your / his / her name? I'm / He's / She's (Pop / Pippa). How old are you / is he / is she? I'm / He's / She's (five). 1

② My day

👁 Look. 📓 Match. 💬 Say.

⊙ Look. 🔍 Find. ◯ Circle. 💬 Say.

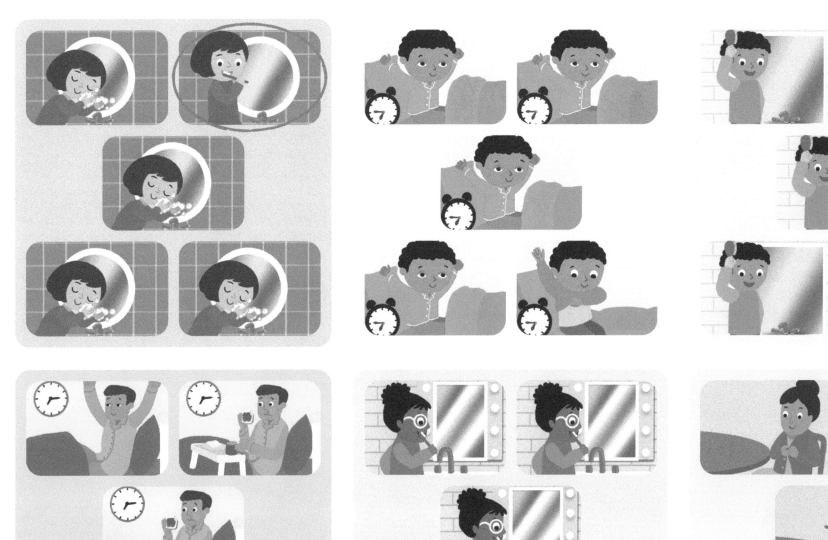

15 **Listen again.** 🖊 **Colour.** ◯ **Trace.** 💬 **Say.**

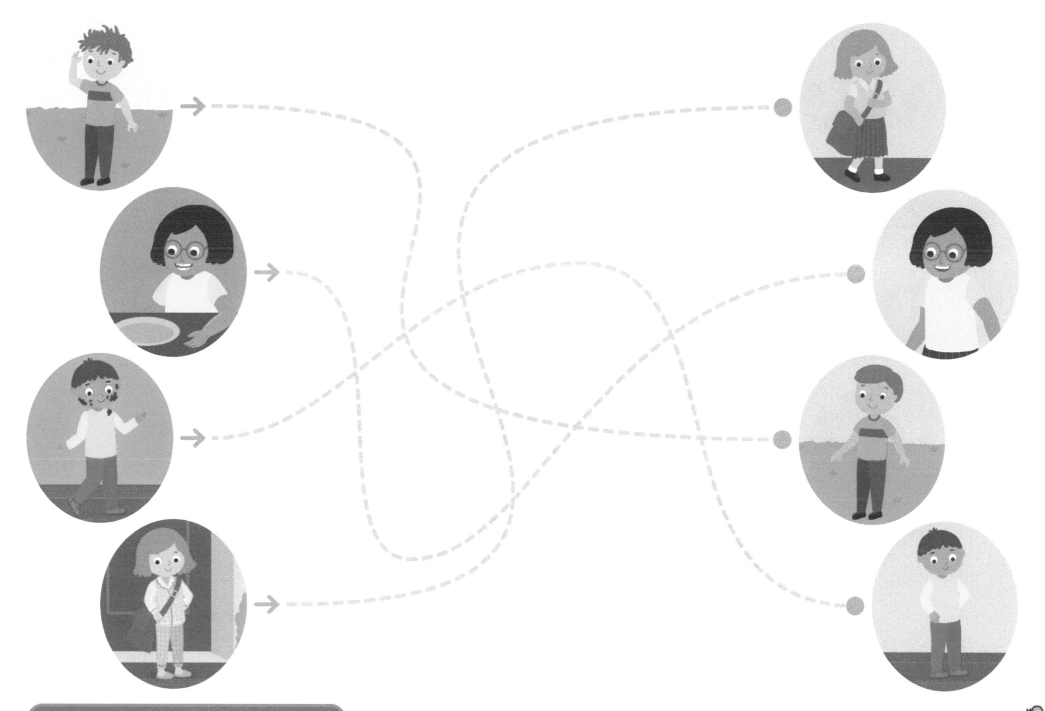

Look. Trace.

👁 Look. 🔍 Find. ⭕ Circle. 💬 Say.

2 Vocabulary practice: *play with friends, have a snack, have a bath, listen to a story, go to bed, have dinner*

👁 Look. 🔍 Find. ⭕ Circle. 💬 Say.

👁 Look. ✋ Count. 📕 Match. 💬 Say.

8 + 1 =

7

4 + 4 =

8

6 + 4 =

9

5 + 2 =

10

🏠 **At home** Make a new adding question.

👁 Look. ⭕ Circle. 💬 Say.

Review

Look. Draw. Say.

2 *I (listen to a story) (every day / in the morning / in the evening).*

 **Point.** **Say.** **Draw.**

Well done!

③ My home

🎧 **20 Listen again.** 👁 **Look.** ⬤ **Stick.** 👆 **Point.**

 Look. 🔍 Find. ◯ Circle. 💬 Say.

⊙ Look. 📖 Match. 💬 Say.

③ **Language practice:** *He / She (sets the table / sweeps the floor / picks up the toys / washes the dishes / makes the bed). I (wash the clothes).*

23 🎧 **Listen again.** ✏️ **Colour.** ⭕ **Trace.** 💬 **Say.**

👁 Look. 👆 Point. ⭕ Circle.

3 Literacy practice: Goldilocks and three bears

◉ Look. 🔍 Find. ✏️ Colour.

Values

⌂ At home

How do you respect other people's things?

Respect other people's things 3

👁 Look. 📖 Match. 💬 Say.

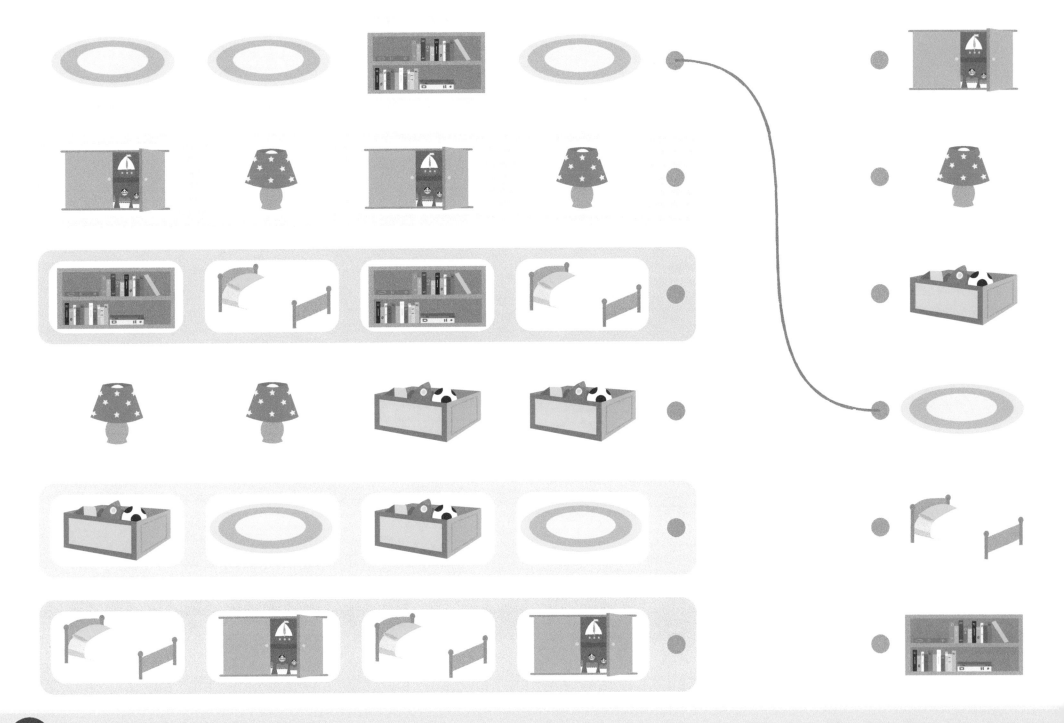

3 Vocabulary practice: *rug, bookcase, cupboard, lamp, bed, toy box*

👁 Look. 🔍 Find. ○ Circle. 💬 Say.

At home

Look in your bedroom. How many sentences can you make?

Numbers

Look. Count. Circle. Say.

(10)

20

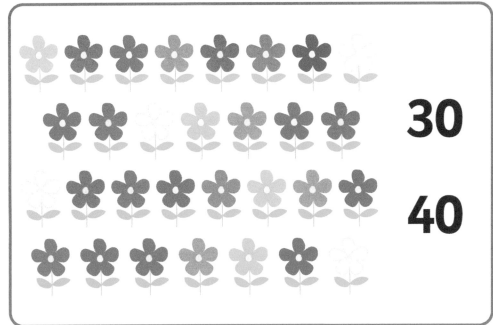

30

40

20

30

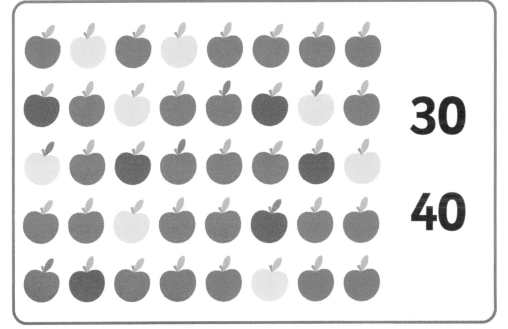

30

40

👁 Look. ✏️ Colour. 💬 Say.

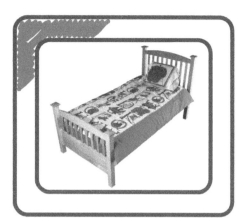

👁 Look. ✏ Draw. 💬 Say.

3 *He / She (washes the dishes). I (sweep the floor) (in the morning).*

Point. Say. Draw.

Well done!

It's (on / under / next to / in) the (bookcase / bed / lamp / cupboard / rug / toy box).

👁 Look. 🔍 Find. 📖 Match. 💬 Say.

✋ Count. 📘 Match. ⭕ Trace. 💬 Say.

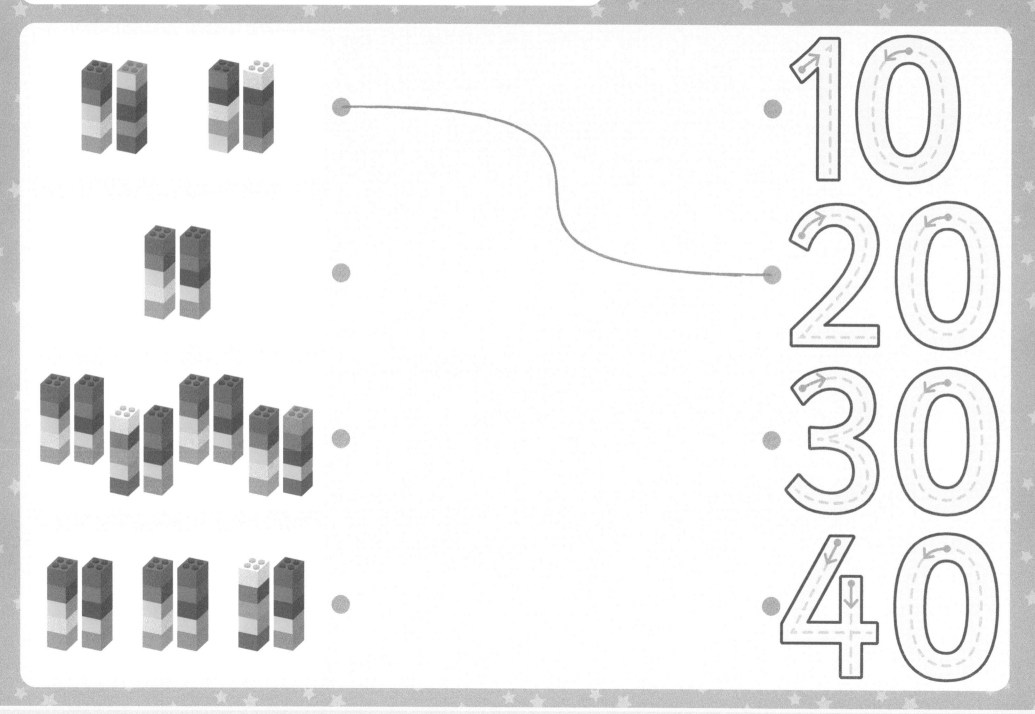

4 My sports

 Look. Match. Say.

👁 Look. 🔍 Find. ⭕ Circle. 💬 Say.

4 **Language practice:** *She's / He's / They're playing (tennis / football / basketball / baseball / badminton / hockey).*

🎧 ³³ **Listen again.** 🔍 **Find.** ⭕ **Circle.** ⭕ **Trace.** 💬 **Say.**

👁 Look. ⬭ Trace.

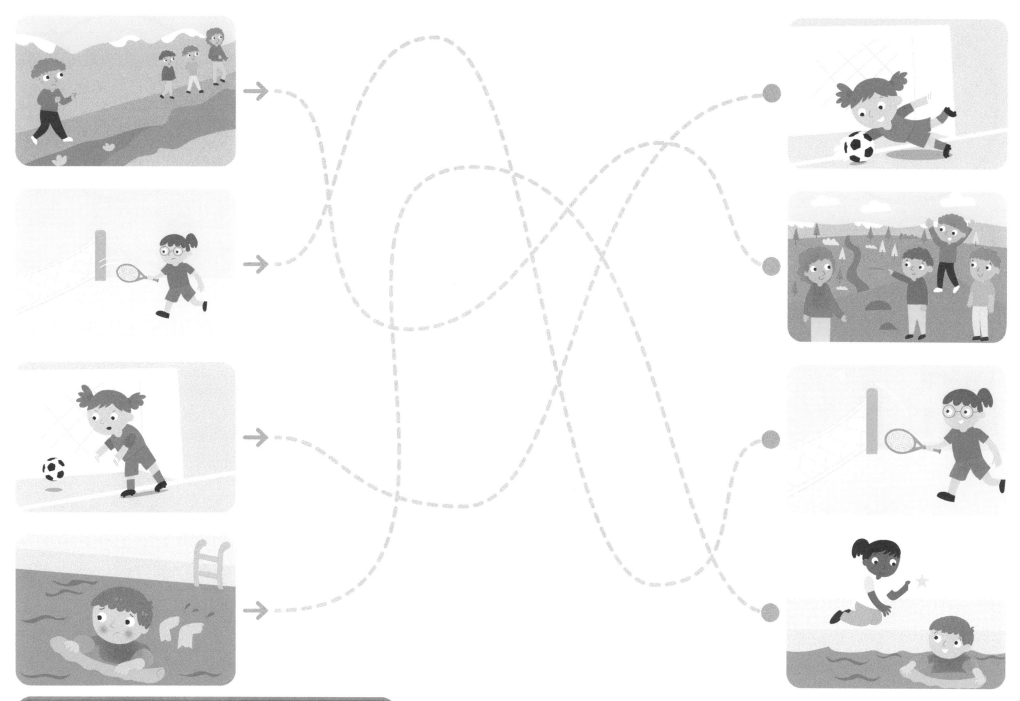

At home When do you persevere?

Look. Match. Say.

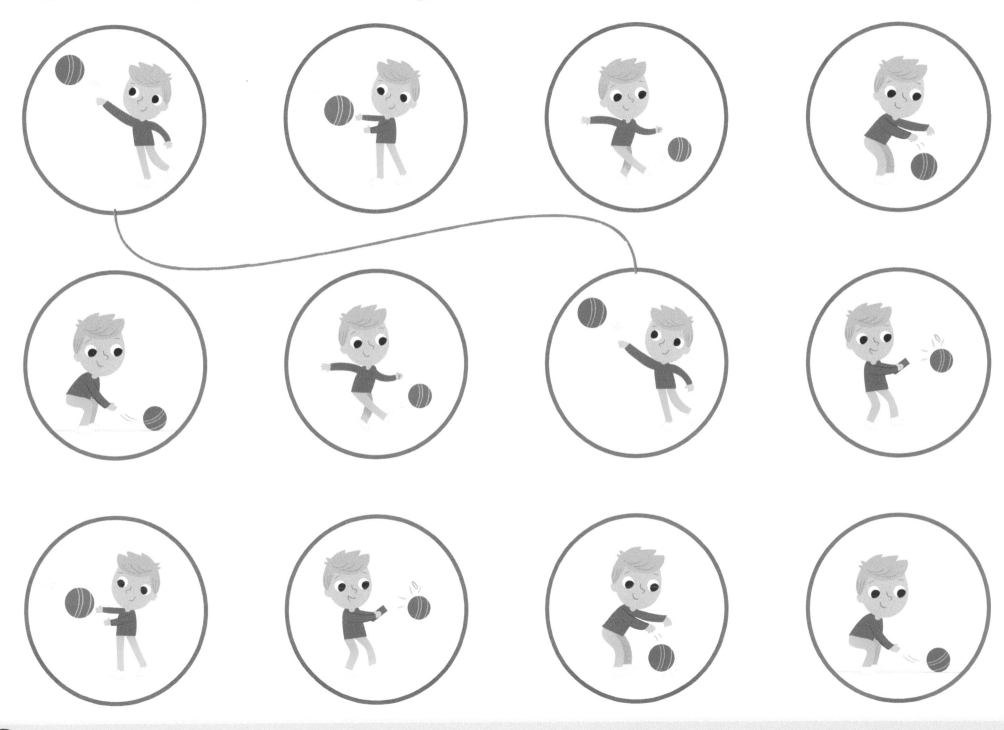

4 **Vocabulary practice:** *throwing, catching, kicking, bouncing, rolling, hitting*

⊙ Look. ✏ Draw. 💬 Say.

Look. Count. Match. Say.

7 – 4 =

5 – 3 =

10 – 5 =

6 – 2 =

2

3

4

5

At home Make a new subtracting question.

👁 **Look.** 🔍 **Find.** ⭕ **Circle.**

👁 **Look.** ✏ **Draw.** 💬 **Say.**

4 *She's / He's / They're (throwing / catching) the ball.*

👆 Point. 💬 Say. ✏️ Draw.

Well done!

⑤ My free time

👁 Look. 🔍 Find. ◯ Circle. 💬 Say.

🏠 **At home**   What do you like doing?

Vocabulary practice: *watching TV, reading books, listening to music, playing video games, cooking, drawing pictures*   5   57

👁 Look. 📖 Match. 💬 Say.

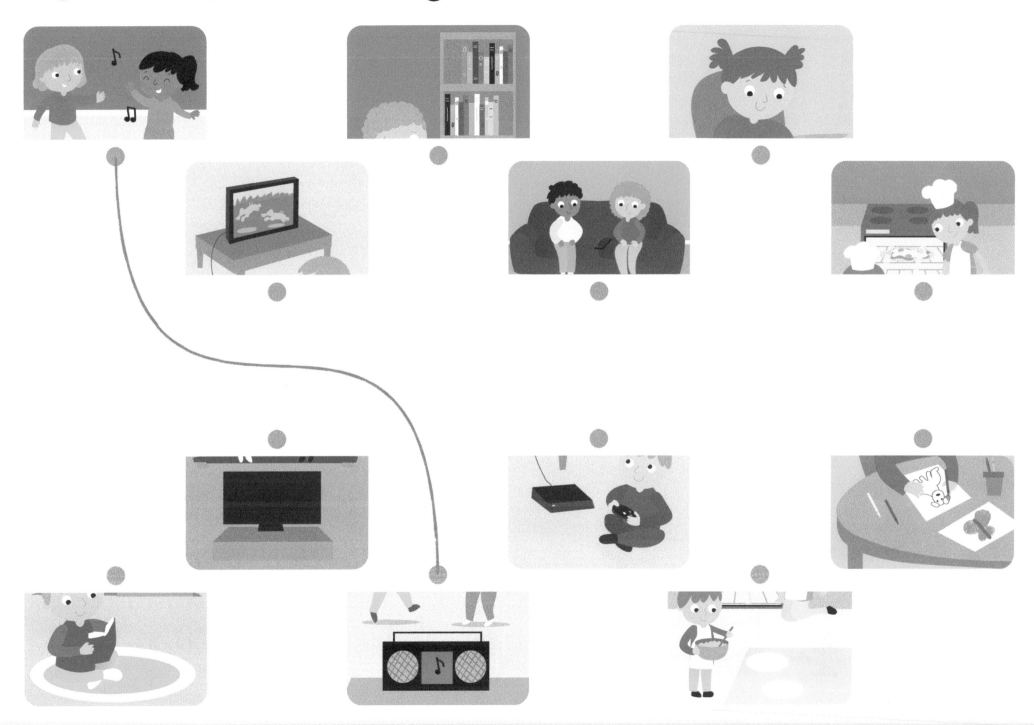

5 **Language practice:** *I / We like (listening to music / playing video games / reading books / watching TV / drawing pictures / cooking).*

42 **Listen again.** 🔍 **Find.** ⭕ **Circle.** ⬭ **Trace.** 💬 **Say.**

🎧⁴³ Listen again. 👁 Look. 1²3 Number.

1

👁 Look. 🔍 Find. ✏️ Draw.

At home

When do you join in and help?

◉ Look. 🔍 Find. ◯ Circle. 💬 Say.

5 **Vocabulary practice:** *play outside, go roller skating, play a board game, play with building blocks, go swimming, play hide-and-seek*

👁 Look. 📘 Match. 💬 Say.

Look. Count. Circle. Say.

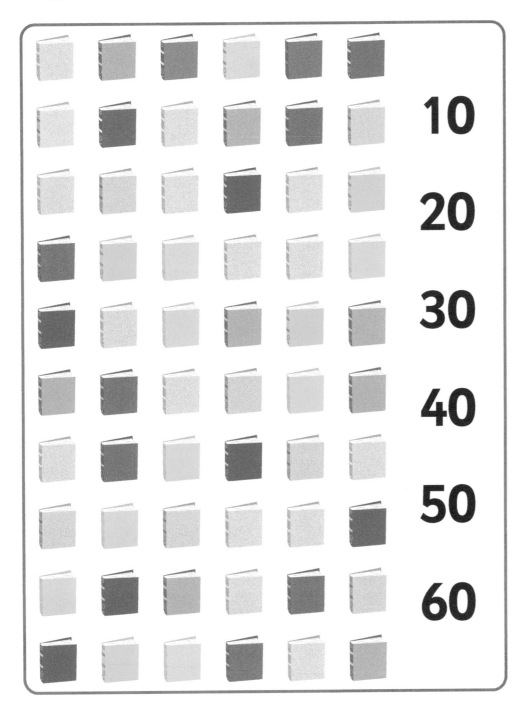

10

20

30

40

50

60

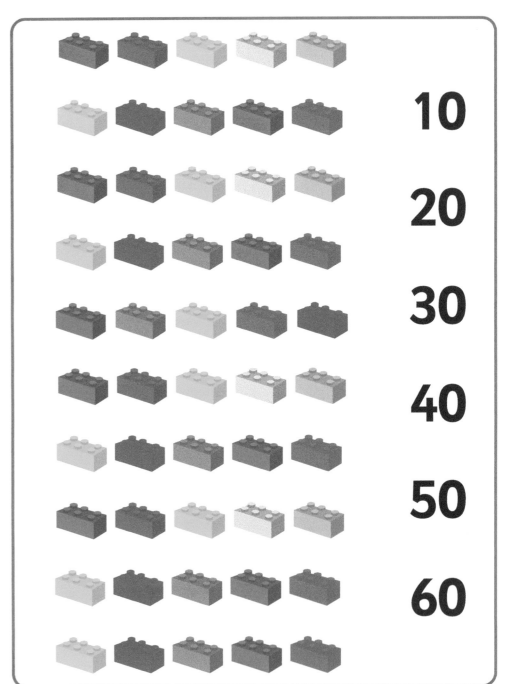

10

20

30

40

50

60

👁 Look. ⭕ Circle. 💬 Say.

👁 **Look.** ✏️ **Draw.** 💬 **Say.**

5 *I / We like (reading books).*

👆 **Point.** 💬 **Say.** ✏️ **Draw.**

Well done!

6 My food

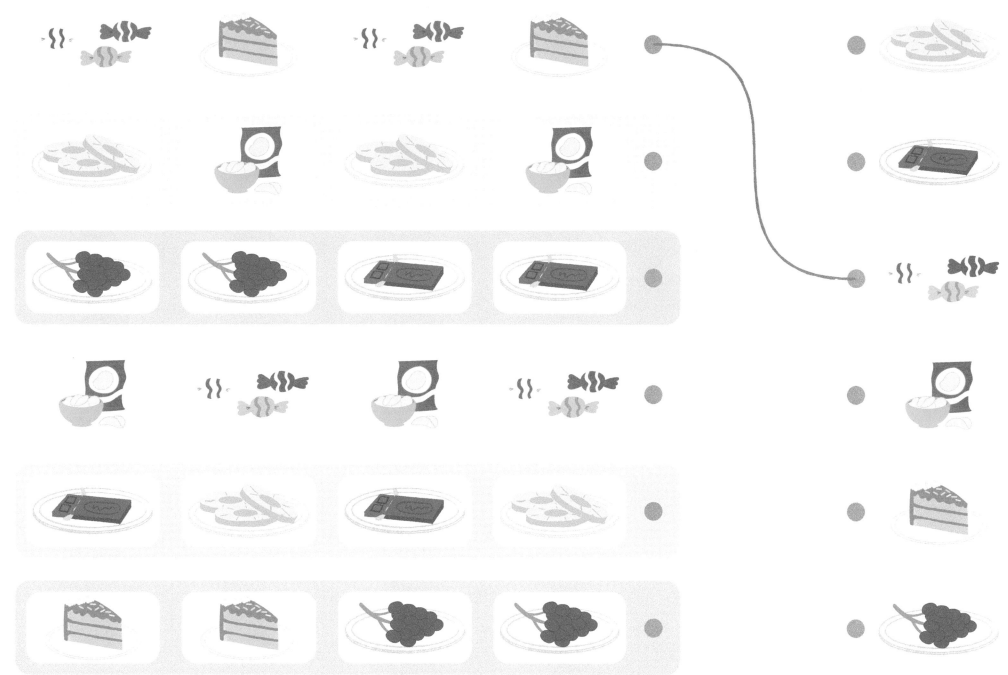 Look. Match. Say.

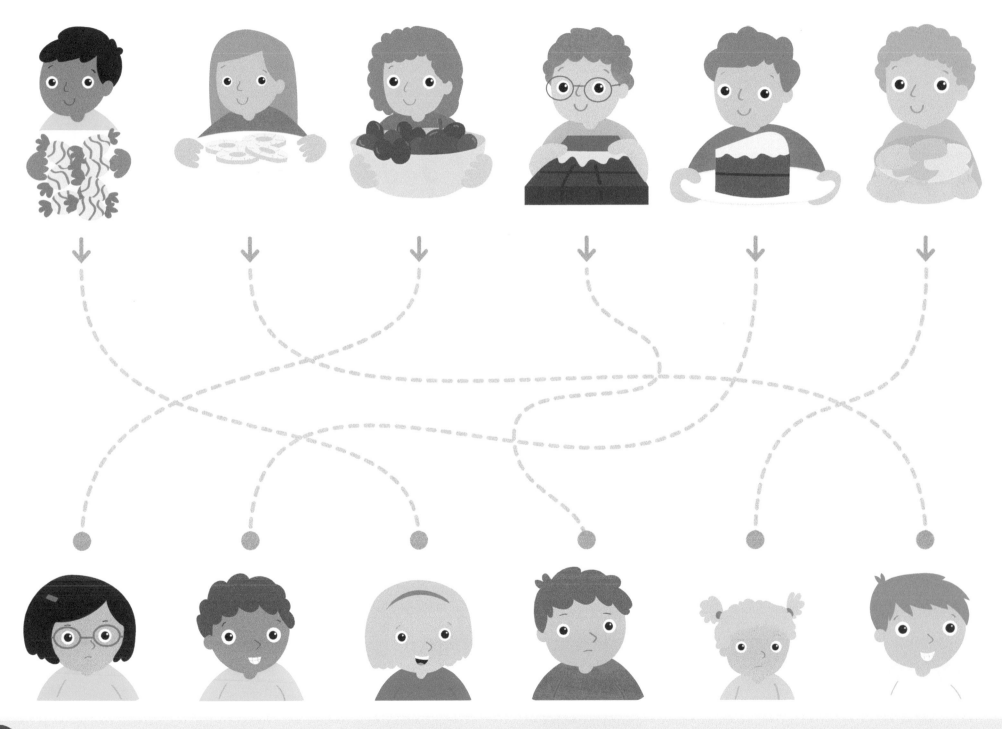

Look. Trace. Say.

6 **Language practice:** *Would you like some (sweets / pineapple / grapes / chocolate / cake / crisps)? Yes, please. / No, thank you.*

🎧⁵¹ **Listen again.** 🔍 **Find.** ◯ **Circle.** ⦿ **Trace.** 🔲 **Say.**

👁 Look. 👆 Point. ⭕ Circle.

6 Literacy practice: Share, Ricky Raccoon!

👁 Look. 🔍 Find. ✏ Colour.

🏠 At home

When do you share?

👁 Look. 📕 Match. 💬 Say.

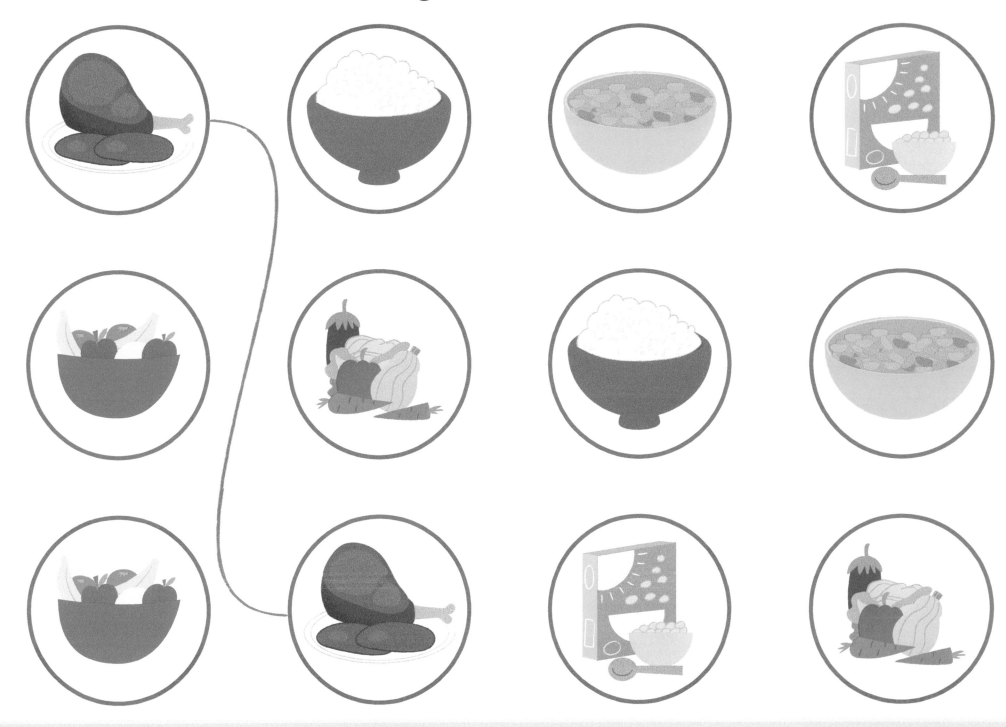

6 Vocabulary practice: *meat, rice, beans, cereal, fruit, vegetables*

👁 Look. 📖 Match. 💬 Say.

 Look. Write. Count. Match.

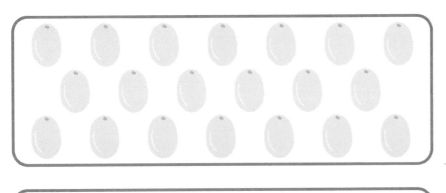

10

20

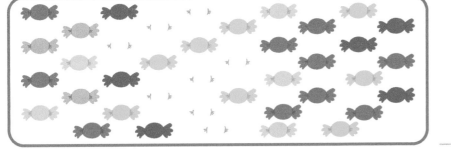

30

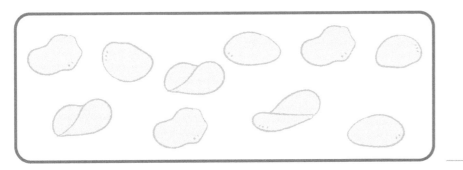

40

50

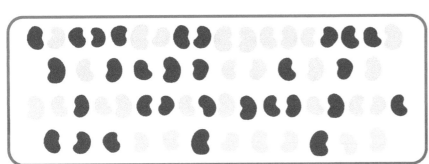

60

👁 **Look.** 🔍 **Find.** ◯ **Circle.** 💬 **Say.**

🏠 **At home** Look in your kitchen. Find sweet, sour and salty foods.

Salty, sour and sweet 6 77

👁 **Look.** ✏ **Draw.** 💬 **Say.**

6 *Would you like some (pineapple)? Yes, please. / No, thank you.*

 Point. Say. Draw.

Well done!

I have (cereal / fruit / meat / rice / vegetables / beans) for (breakfast / lunch / dinner). 6

👁 Look. 🔍 Find. 📖 Match. 💬 Say.

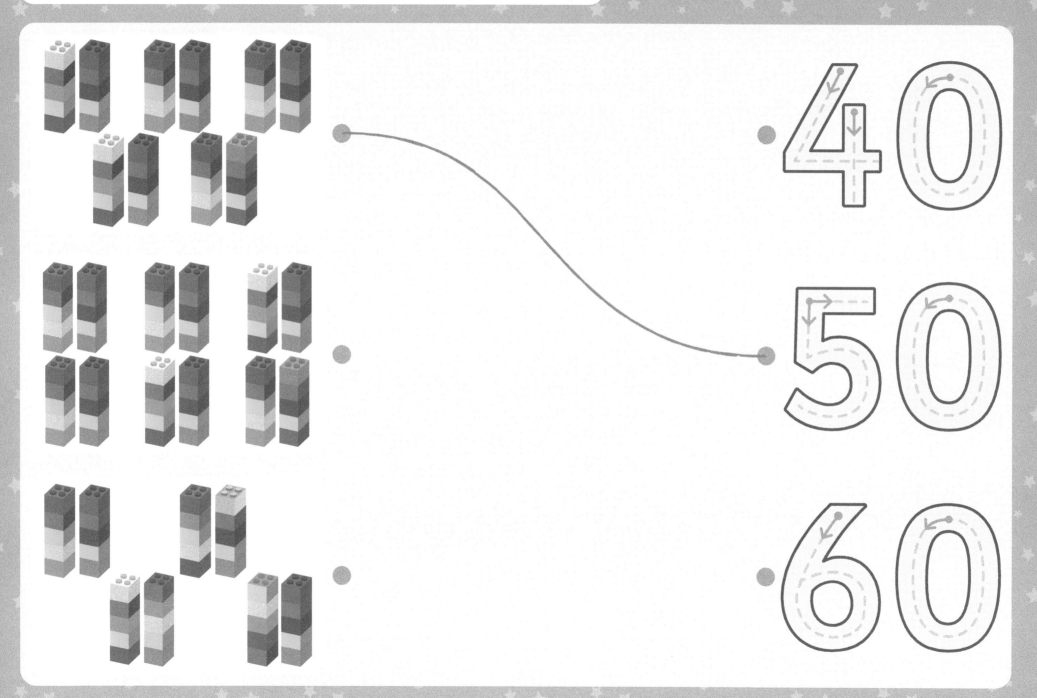

7 Animals

7 Unit topic introduction: Song practice

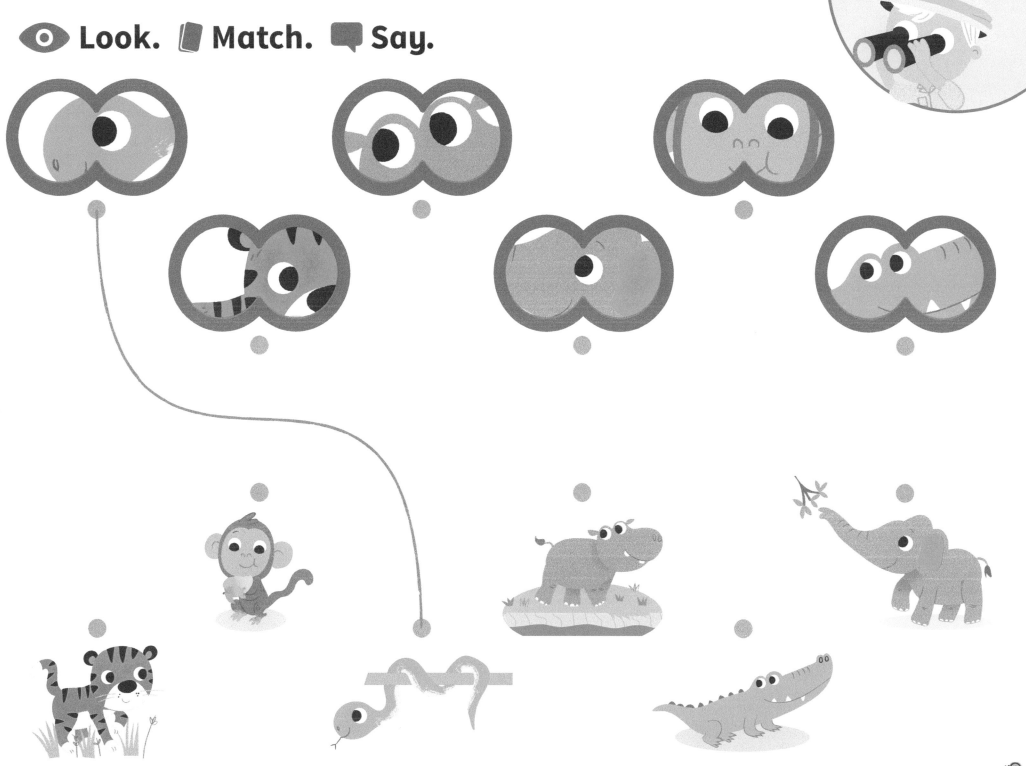

👁 **Look.** 📖 **Match.** 💬 **Say.**

👁 Look. ✋ Count. ✏ Write. 💬 Say.

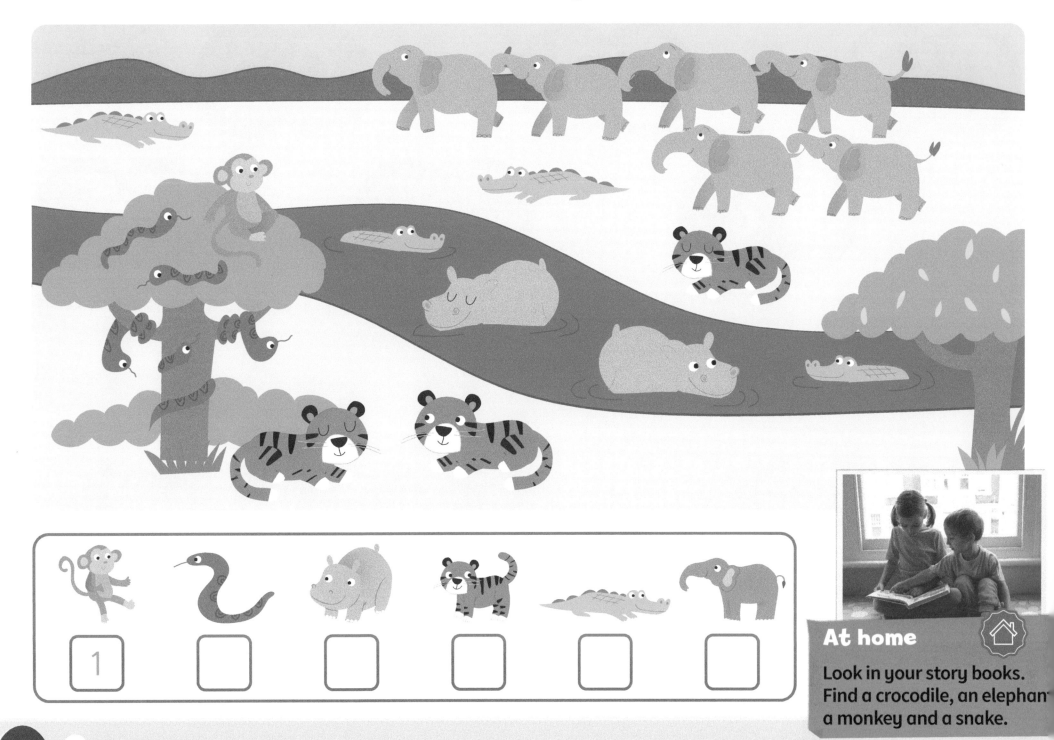

At home

Look in your story books. Find a crocodile, an elephant, a monkey and a snake.

7 **Language practice:** *There's a (monkey). There are (five) (snakes / hippos / tigers / crocodiles). There are lots of (elephants).*

🎧 **Listen again.** ✏️ **Colour.** ⬭ **Trace.** 💬 **Say.**

👁 Look. ⭕ Trace.

👁 Look. 🔍 Find. ⭕ Circle. 💬 Say.

7 Vocabulary practice: *giraffes, zebras, ducks, lizards, spiders, parrots*

🏠 **At home** Talk to a friend. Ask *Do you like giraffes? Do you like ducks?*

Look. 👁 Find. 🔍 Circle. ⭕ Say. 💬

Numbers

🐛🐛🐛🐛🐛🐛🐛	**10**
🐛🐛🐛🐛🐛🐛🐛	**20**
🐛🐛🐛🐛🐛🐛🐛	**30**
🐛🐛🐛🐛🐛🐛🐛	**40**
🐛🐛🐛🐛🐛🐛🐛	**50**
🐛🐛🐛🐛🐛🐛🐛	**60**
🐛🐛🐛🐛🐛🐛🐛	**70**
🐛🐛🐛🐛🐛🐛🐛	**80**

🦛🦛🦛🦛🦛🦛🦛	**10**
🦛🦛🦛🦛🦛🦛🦛	**20**
🦛🦛🦛🦛🦛🦛🦛	**30**
🦛🦛🦛🦛🦛🦛🦛	**40**
🦛🦛🦛🦛🦛🦛🦛	**50**
🦛🦛🦛🦛🦛🦛🦛	**60**
🦛🦛🦛🦛🦛🦛🦛	**70**
🦛🦛🦛🦛🦛🦛🦛	**80**

👁 **Look.** 🔍 **Find.** ◯ **Circle.** 💬 **Say.**

land

land and water

water

Look. Draw. Say.

7 *They're (lizards). They've got (long tails) and (short legs).*

 **Point.** **Say.** **Draw.**

Well done!

There's a (crocodile / tiger / hippo). There are (four) (monkeys). There are lots of (snakes / elephants).

7

8 Plants

67 Listen again. 👁 Look. ◯ Stick. 👆 Point.

👁 Look. 📖 Match. 💬 Say.

🏠 **At home** Look outside. What can you see?

Vocabulary practice: *seeds, rain, plants, garden, soil, sun* 8 95

  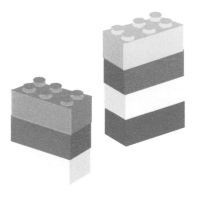

👁 **Look.** ◯ **Circle.** 💬 **Say.**

8 **Language practice:** *Plants need (sun / rain / soil).*

🎧 **⁷⁰ Listen again.** 🔍 **Find.** ⭕ **Circle.** ⭕ **Trace.** 💬 **Say.**

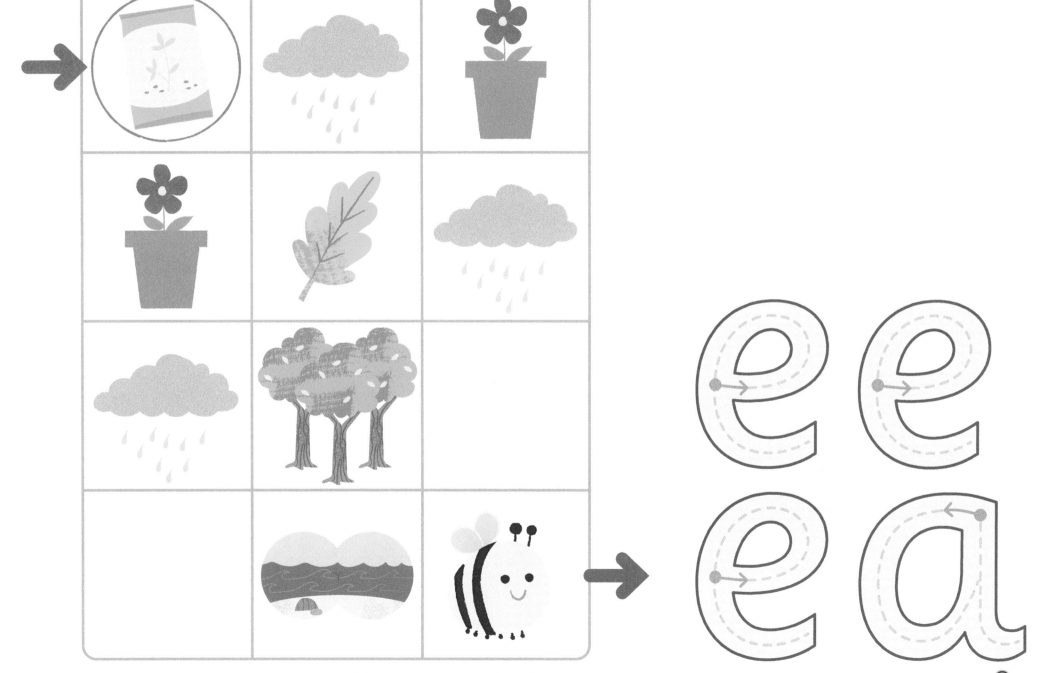

🎧 71 Listen again. 👁 Look. 🔢 Number.

1

👁 Look. 🔍 Find. ✏ Colour.

🏠 **At home**

When do you work together?

👁 Look. 🔍 Find. ⭕ Circle. 💬 Say.

8 *Vocabulary practice: beautiful, ugly, clean, dirty, old, new*

👁 Look. 🔍 Find. ⭕ Circle. 💬 Say.

👁 **Look.** ✋ **Count.** 📖 **Match.** 💬 **Say.**

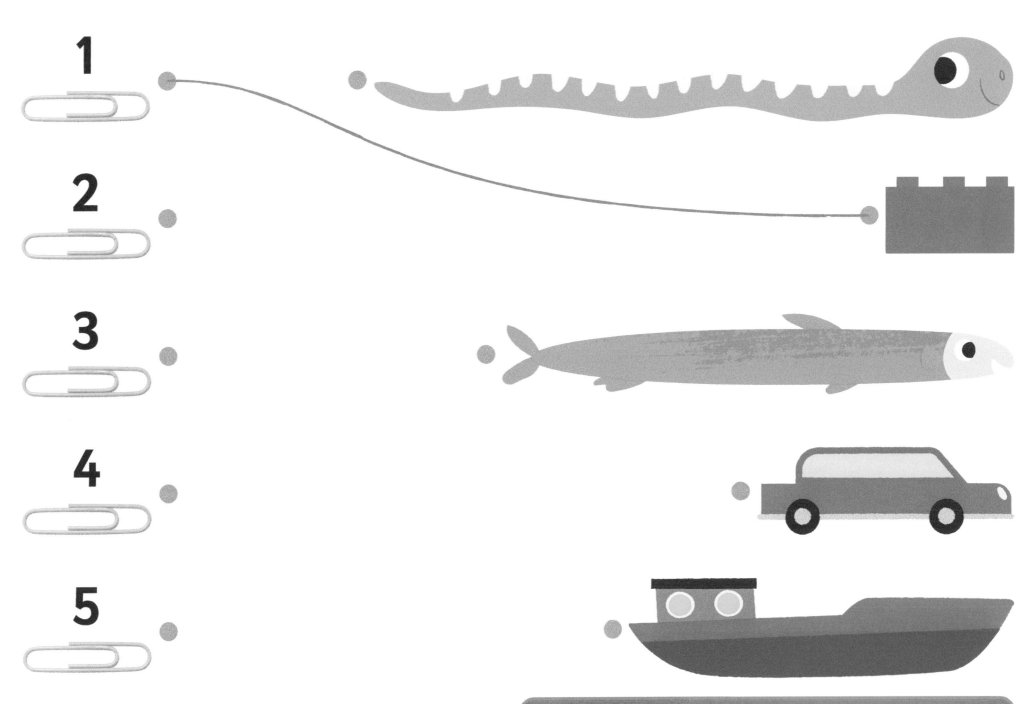

1

2

3

4

5

🏠 **At home** Measure three things with a paperclip.

👁 Look. 📙 Match. 💬 Say.

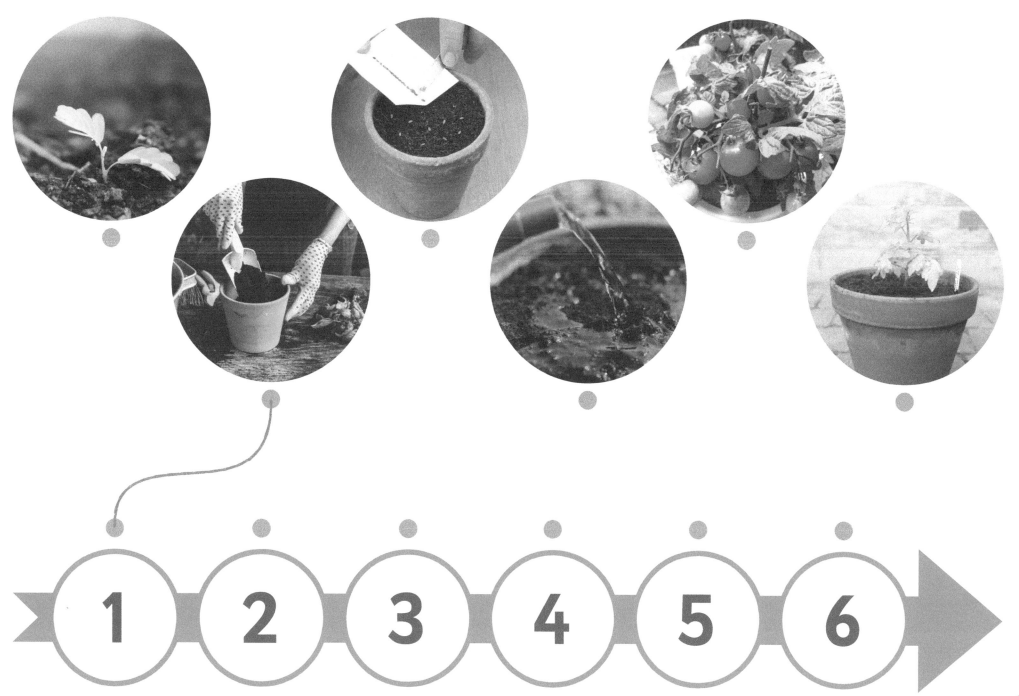

👁 Look. ✏ Draw. 💬 Say.

8 *What (beautiful) (flowers)! What (an old) (tree)!*

👆 **Point.** 💬 **Say.** ✏️ **Draw.**

Well done!

garden, seeds, plants; What do plants need? Plants need (sun / rain / soil). 8

⑨ My town

👁 Look. 📖 Match. 💬 Say.

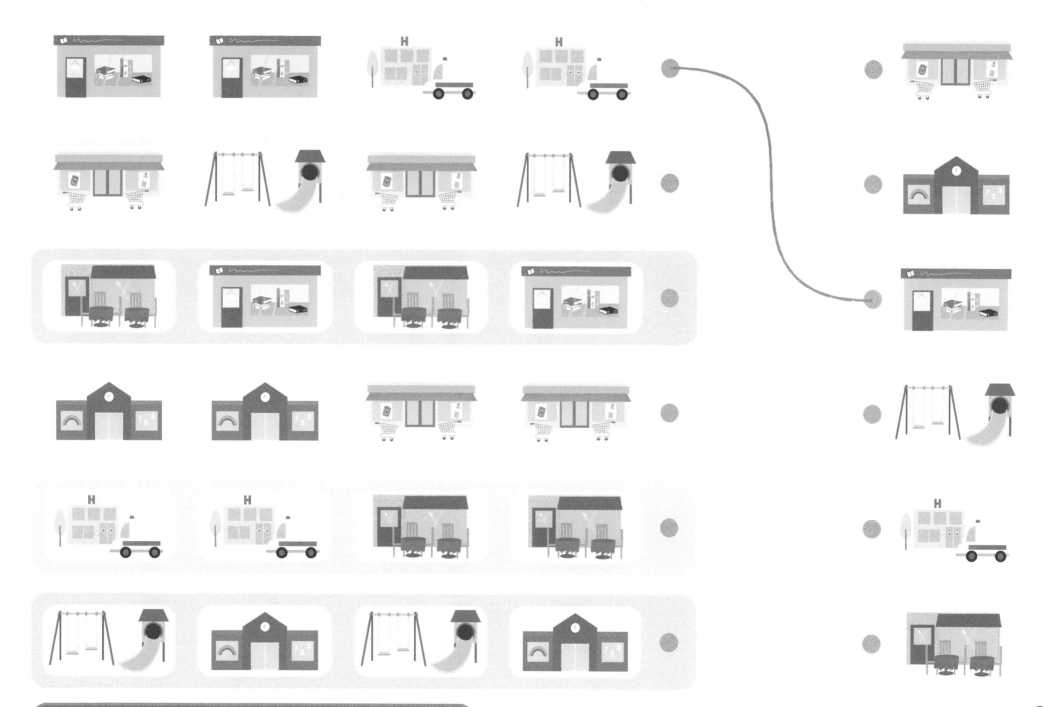

Look. Trace. Say.

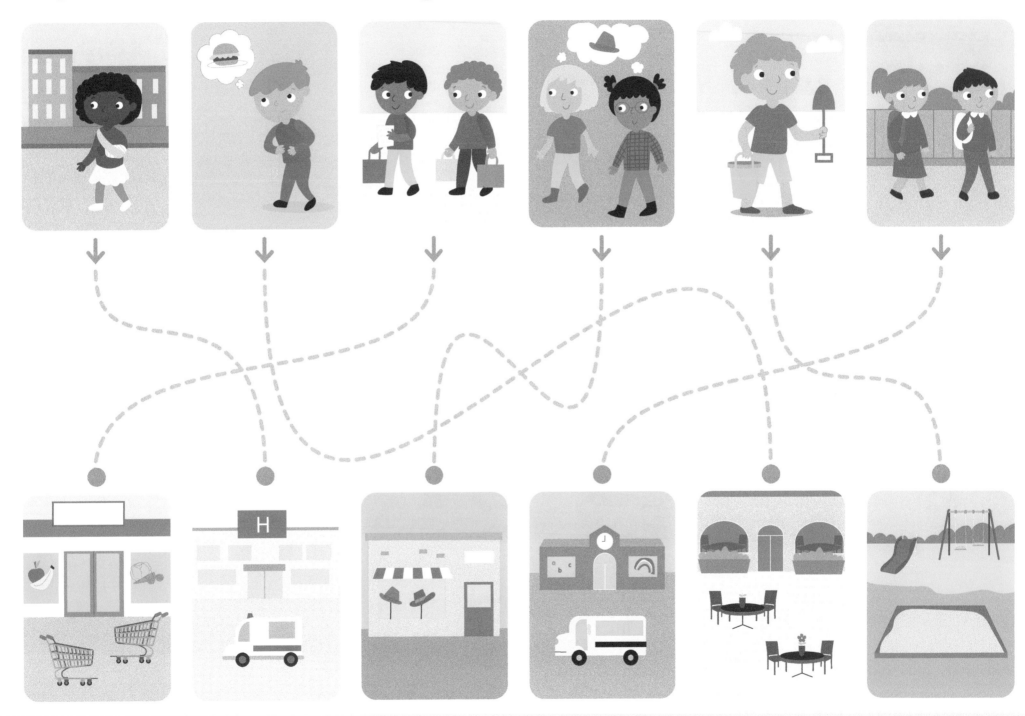

9 **Language practice:** *Where are you / are we going? I'm / We're going to the (supermarket / hospital / shop / school / restaurant / playground).*

🎧 78 **Listen again.** ✏️ **Colour.** ⭕ **Trace.** 💬 **Say.**

👁 Look. 👆 Point. ⭕ Circle.

9 *Literacy practice:* Big-city cat and small-town cat

👁 Look. ⬭ Trace.

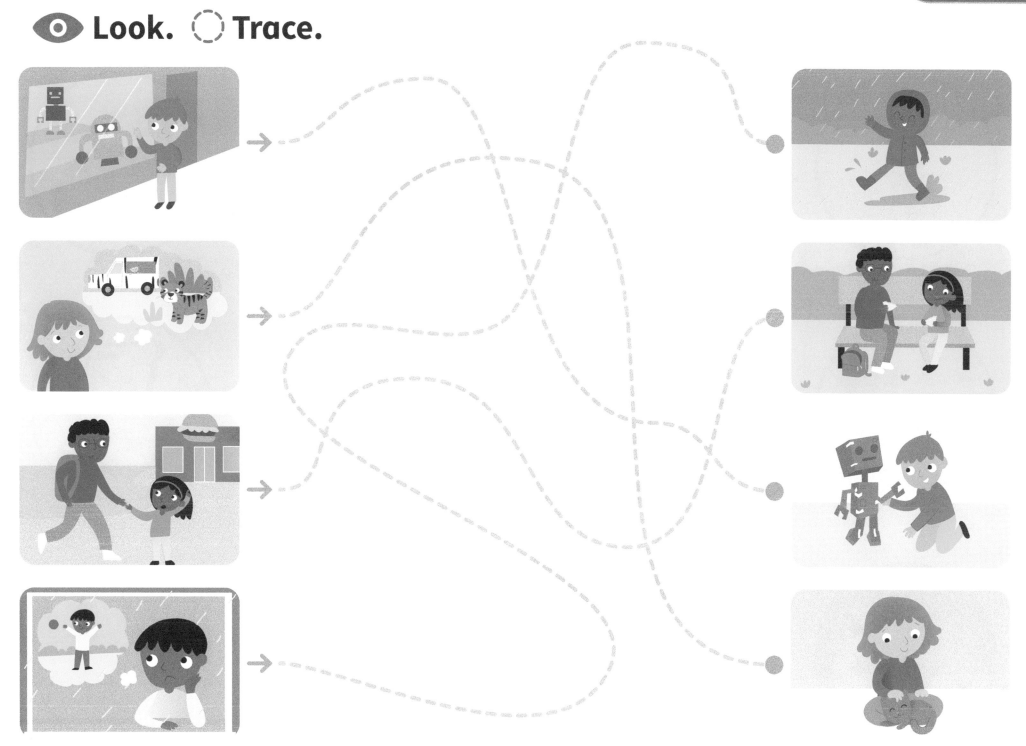

◉ Look. 📖 Match. 💬 Say.

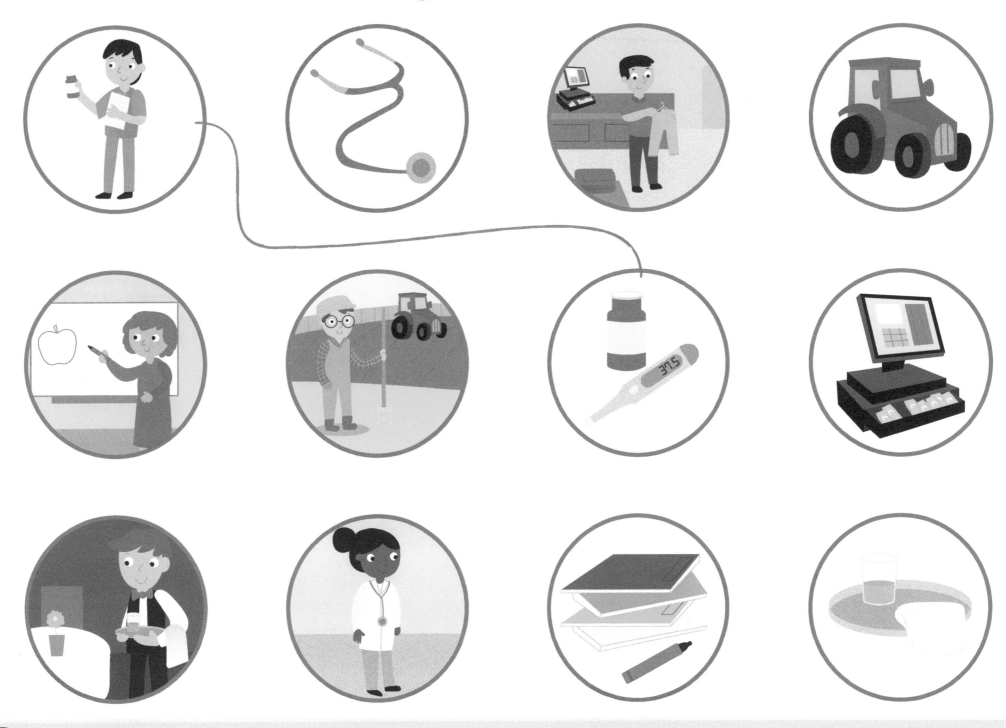

⊙ Look. ○ Circle. 💬 Say.

👁 Look. ✋ Count. ◯ Circle. 💬 Say.

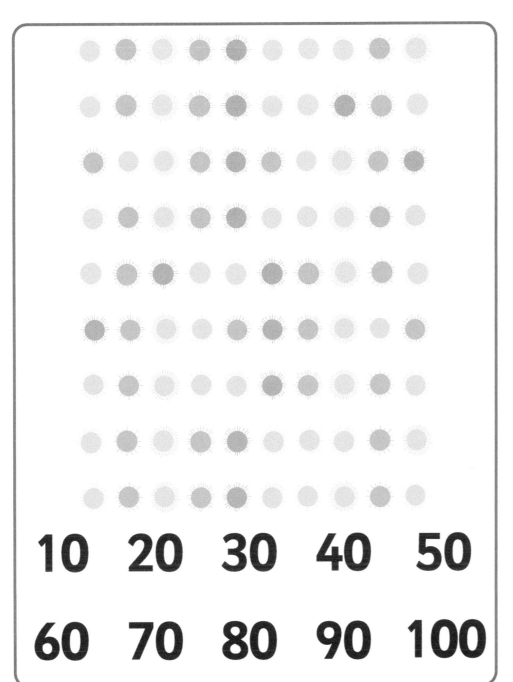

10   20   30   40   50
60   70   80   90   100

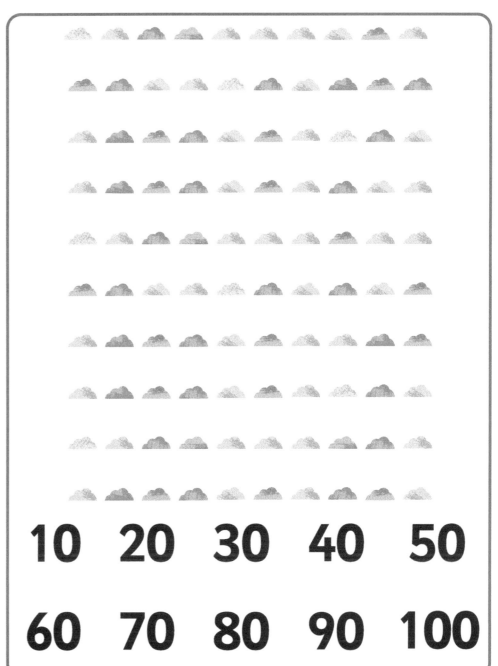

10   20   30   40   50
60   70   80   90   100

🏠 **At home**   How many fingers are in your family? Count.

👁 **Look.** 🔍 **Find.** ◯ **Circle.** 💬 **Say.**

   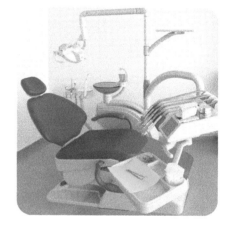

Look. Draw. Say.

9 *Where are you / we going? I'm / We're going to the (shop).*

👆 **Point.** 💬 **Say.** ✏️ **Draw.**

Well done!

ay

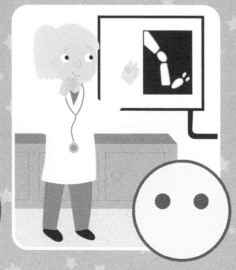 

A (shop assistant / nurse / waiter / teacher / doctor) works (in) a (hospital). A (farmer) works (on) a (farm).

👁 Look. 🔍 Find. 📖 Match. 💬 Say.

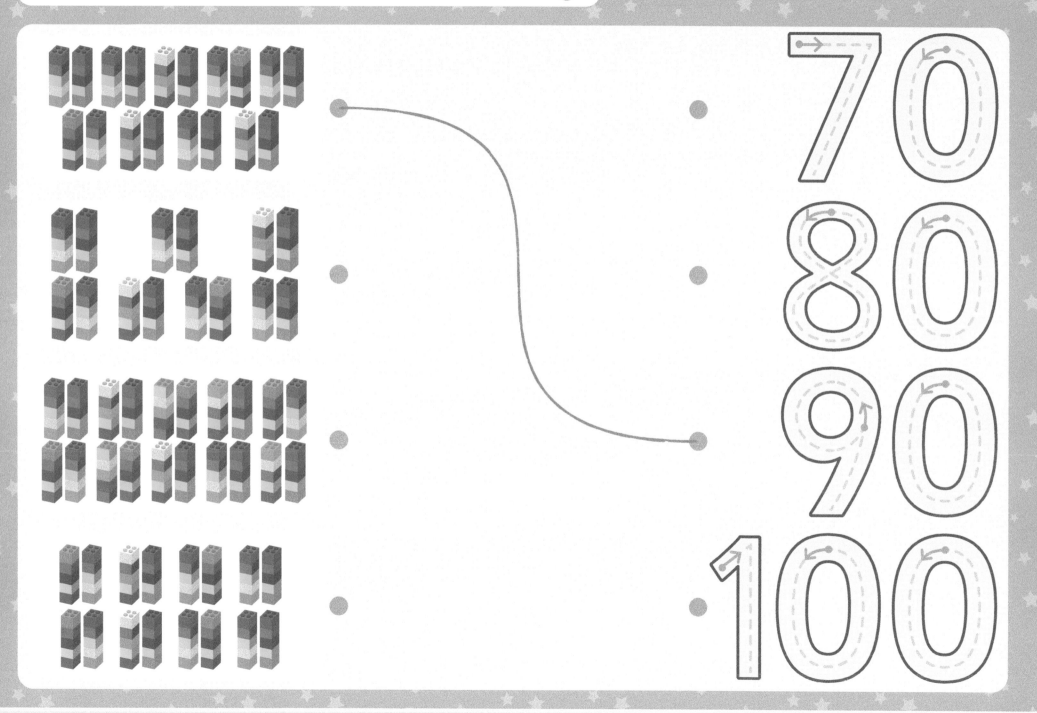

Count. Match. Trace. Say.

70
80
90
100

Thanks and Acknowledgements

The publishers and authors would like to thank the following contributors:
Book design and page make-up by Blooberry Design.
Cover design by Blooberry Design.
In-house editing by Zara Hutchinson-Goncalves.
Freelance editing by Catherine Ball and Stephanie Howard.
Audio recording and production by Ian Harker.
Original songs and chants by Robert Lee.
Songs and chants production by Jake Carter.

The authors and publishers acknowledge the following sources of copyright material and are grateful for the permissions granted. While every effort has been made, it has not always been possible to identify the sources of all the material used, or to trace all copyright holders. If any omissions are brought to our notice, we will be happy to include the appropriate acknowledgements on reprinting and in the next update to the digital edition, as applicable.

Key: U = Unit.

Photography

All photos are sourced from Getty Images.
U1: imagenavi; **U2:** aldomurillo/E+; David De Lossy/DigitalVision; PeopleImages/iStock/Getty Images Plus; BananaStock; Wavebreakmedia/iStock/Getty Images Plus; Nick David/Photodisc; **U3:** Johannes Mann/The Image Bank; Imgorthand/E+; PhotoAlto/Antoine Arraou; scibak/E+; Lawrence Manning/Corbis; -slav-/iStock/Getty Images Plus; MediaProduction/E+; kertlis/iStock/Getty Images Plus; Sollina Images; jodiejohnson/iStock/Getty Images Plus; John Keeble/Moment; Image Source/DigitalVision; tiler84/iStock / Getty Images Plus; pagadesign/iStock / Getty Images Plus; SKrow/E+; **U5:** katleho Seisa/E+; Kemal Can Habip/EyeEm; Image Source; ajr_images/iStock/Getty Images Plus; Tuul & Bruno Morandi/The Image Bank; Stefan Cristian Cioata/Moment; David Blaikie/Moment; Witthaya Prasongsin/Moment; Nongkran_ch/iStock/Getty Images Plus; Liliya Kulianionak/iStock/Getty Images Plus; Alexander Friedrich/500px; Ronnie Kaufman/DigitalVision; Simon Eeman/EyeEm; **U6:** Sally Anscombe/Stone; Tim UR/iStock/Getty Images Plus; Veeravong Komalamena/EyeEm; vmenshov/iStock/Getty Images Plus; Pineapple Studio/iStock/Getty Images Plus; baibaz/iStock/Getty Images Plus; Kristin Duvall/The Image Bank; OKRAD/iStock/Getty Images Plus; RedHelga/iStock/Getty Images Plus; chonessiStock/Getty Images Plus; **U7:** Maria Spann/Photographer's Choice RF; Magnus Larsson/iStock/Getty Images Plus; isoft/E+; BarbAnna/Moment; Reinhard Dirscherl/The Image bank; Richard A. Whittaker/Moment; Giampaolo Cianella/Moment; Manoj Shah/Stone; GlobalP/iStock/Getty Images Plus; Edmund Lowe Photography/Moment; fenkieandreas/iStock/Getty Images Plus; Andreas Speich/EyeEm; Cristian H. Gomez/EyeEm; **U8:** Mint Images; tortoon/iStock/Getty Images Plus; Sarah Palmer/Moment; Lindeblad, Matilda; Nora Carol Photography/Moment; Johner Images; valentinrussanov/E+; Jetta Productions Inc.; DigitalVision; cocorattanakorn/iStock/Getty Images Plus; Steve Hamilton/Photolibrary; DigiPub/Moment; Ashley Jouhar/Photographer's Choice RF; FreshSplash/E+; Guido Mieth/DigitalVision; **U9:** andresr/E+; gerenme/iStock/Getty Images Plus; brankokosteski/iStock/Getty Images Plus; vm/E+; Sam Edwards/OJO Images; Robert Daly/OJO Images; Sitade/iStock/Getty Images Plus; Mint Images; Monty Rakusen/Cultura; artisteer/iStock/Getty Images Plus; Image Source; georgeclerk/iStock/Getty Images Plus; kali9/E+; Jetta Productions Inc./DigitalVision; mokee81/iStock/Getty Images Plus.

Illustrations

Amy Zhing; Beatriz Castro; Begoña Corbalán; Dean Gray; Isabel Nicolle; Louise Forshaw and Collaborate artists; Noopur Thakur.
Cover illustration by Collaborate Agency.